Shilly  y:

Inside the Mind of a Master Procrastinator
and
Recommended Daily Routine for Peak Productivity.

by

Emma T. Phils

Shilly Shally

Copyright © by **Emma T. Phils** 2022. All rights reserved. Before this document is duplicated or reproduced in any manner, the publisher's consent must be gained. Therefore, the contents within can neither be stored electronically, transferred, nor kept in a database. Neither in Part nor full can the document be copied, scanned, faxed, or retained without approval from the publisher or creator.

TABLE OF CONTENT

Introduction 4

Chapter 1 6

What is Procrastination? 6

Chapter 2 11

Inside the mind of a master procrastinator 11

Chapter 3 17

Why people Procrastinate 17

Chapter 4 61

Procrastination-Action Line 61

Chapter 5 70

Recommended Daily Routine, for Peak Productivity
.... 70

Conclusion 78

Introduction

If you're a procrastinator, then you've undoubtedly questioned yourself at some time "why do I postpone so much?" or "why do I keep postponing even though I know that it's harmful to me?". These are key questions, as knowing why you postpone is vital if you want to find out how to quit doing it.

Specifically, you would get inside the head of a master procrastinator and you would see a full list of reasons why individuals procrastinate, based on decades of study on the issue. Furthermore, you will discover how this knowledge may help you find out why you procrastinate, and how you can utilize it to effectively overcome your procrastination.

Procrastination is an issue we have all battled at one time in our lives. we've been fighting with postponing, avoiding, and procrastinating on problems that are important to us.

Shilly Shally

During our more productive times, when we briefly find out how to stop procrastinating, we feel content and successful. We're going to talk about how to make those uncommon moments of production more normal. The objective of this book is to break down the science behind why we procrastinate, give proven frameworks you can use to conquer procrastination, and explore valuable methods that will make it simpler to take action.

Note that this book is vast, because procrastination is a complicated issue, that various individuals suffer for various reasons. However, don't be discouraged; feel free to peruse this book, particularly when it comes to the list of reasons why people delay, and concentrate on the topics that are the most important to you.

Chapter 1

What is Procrastination?

Human beings have been procrastinating for eons. The issue is so ageless that ancient Greek philosophers like Socrates and Aristotle devised a name to characterize this sort of behaviour: Akrasia.

"Akrasia is the condition of behaving against your better judgment. It is doing one thing even if you know you should do something other. Loosely translated, one may argue that akrasia is procrastination or a lack of self-control".

Here's a contemporary definition:
The dictionary definition: Procrastination is the act of delaying or postponing a job or group of tasks: your first suggestion is to prevent procrastination.

Shilly Shally

So, whether referring to it as procrastination or akrasia or anything else, it is the force that keeps you from following through on what you set out to achieve.

Why Do We Procrastinate?

Ok, definitions are fine and all, but why do we procrastinate? What goes on in the brain that drives us to avoid the things we know we should be doing?

This is an excellent opportunity to introduce some science into our debate. Behavioural psychology study has identified a phenomenon called "time inconsistency," which helps explain why procrastination tends to suck us in despite our good intentions. Time inconsistency refers to the propensity of the human brain to value present rewards more highly than future rewards. Economists have a similar notion, which they term "hyperbolic discounting."

The easiest way grasping this is by assuming you have two selves: your Present and future selves. When you

Shilly Shally

establish objectives for yourself — like losing weight, publishing a book, or learning a language — you are essentially creating preparations for your Future Self. You are visualizing what you want your life to look like in the future. Researchers have shown that when you think about your Future Self, it is relatively simple for your brain to perceive the worth of doing activities with long-term advantages. The Future Self prioritizes long-term gains.

Although the Future Self may make objectives, but only the Present Self take actions. When the time comes for decision making, you are no longer making choices for your Future Self. Now you're in the present moment, and your brain is thinking about your Present Self. Researchers have determined that the Present Self truly enjoys rapid satisfaction, not long-term return.

So, the Present and the Future Self are frequently in conflict with one another. The Future Self wants to be slim and fit, while the Present Self craves a doughnut. Sure, everyone knows you should eat properly now to prevent getting overweight in 10 years. But effects like an increased risk for diabetes or heart failure remain years distant.

Similarly, many young people recognize that saving for retirement in their 20s and 30s is vital, but the advantage of doing so is decades off. It is a lot simpler for the Present Self to recognize the value in purchasing a new pair of shoes than in socking aside $100 for 70-year-old you. (If you're wondering, there are some very excellent evolutionary reasons why our brain rates immediate rewards more highly than long-term gains.)

This is one reason why you could go to bed feeling eager to make a difference in your life, but when you wake up you find yourself relapsing back into old behaviors. Your brain appreciates long-term gains when they are in the future (tomorrow), but it prefers instant satisfaction when it comes to the current moment (today).

When it comes to particular reasons why individuals delay, in terms of demotivating and impeding circumstances, the following are among the most common

Shilly Shally

- Abstract aims.
- Outcomes that are distant in the future.
- A detachment with our future selves.
- Feeling overwhelmed.
- Anxiety.
- Task aversion.
- Perfectionism.
- Fear (e.g., of failure, assessment, or negative feedback) (e.g., of failure, evaluation, or negative feedback).
- Perceived loss of control.
- ADHD.
- Depression.
- Lack of motivation.
- Lack of energy.
- Sensation seeking.

To successfully deal with procrastination, you need to figure out why you procrastinate and how your procrastination is preventing you from achieving your goals, so you can formulate a concrete plan of action based on appropriate anti-procrastination techniques, that will help you deal with your reason for procrastination.

Chapter 2

Inside the mind of a master procrastinator

Who would guess that after decades of battle with procrastination, the dictionary, of all places, would contain the remedy?

Avoid procrastinating. So gorgeous and elegant in its simplicity.
The issue the dictionary doesn't grasp is that for a true procrastinator, procrastinating isn't optional—it's something they don't know how not to do.

To understand why procrastinators procrastinate, let's start by studying a non-procrastinators brain:

A non-procrastinator brain - has a Logical decision maker that creates and plans out every specific choice of current and future duty.

Shilly Shally

While the brain of a procrastinator - It appears the logical decision Maker in the procrastinator's brain is living with an undesirable roommate called Instant Gratification,

which makes it harder for the rational decision maker to execute his job properly.

The reality is, Instant Gratification should be the least in command of decisions—he thinks only about the now, dismissing lessons from the past and discarding the future totally. He focuses himself entirely on increasing the comfort and pleasure of the current moment. He doesn't understand the Logical Decision-Maker any more than the Logical Decision-Maker knows him—why would we continue doing this jog, he wonders, when we could quit, which would feel better. Why would we practice that instrument when it isn't fun? Why would we ever utilize a computer for work when the internet is sitting right there wanting to be played with? He believes he's got it all figured out—if you eat when you're hungry, sleep when you're sleepy and don't do anything challenging, you're fairly successful. The procrastinator's dilemma is that he

Shilly Shally

lives in the human world, making Instant Gratification a highly unqualified navigator of the human world. Meanwhile, the Logical Decision-Maker, who was trained to make rational decisions, not to deal with competition over the controls, doesn't know how to put up an effective fight with instant Gratification—he just feels worse and worse about himself the more he fails and the more the suffering procrastinator whose head he's in berates him. It's a disaster. And with instant Gratification in control, the procrastinator finds himself spending a lot of time in a Dark realm.

The Dark Realm is a location every procrastinator knows well. It's a location where leisure activities happen at times when leisure activities are not meant to be occurring. The joy you experience in the Dark Realm isn't truly fun since it's utterly undeserved and the air is filled with guilt, anxiety, self-hatred, and dread. Sometimes the Logical Decision Maker puts his foot down and refuses to let you spend time doing typical leisure things, and because Instant Gratification sure as hell isn't going to let you work, you

Shilly Shally

find yourself in a bizarre purgatory of unusual activities where everyone loses.

And the poor Logical Decision-Maker simply mopes, trying to figure out how he allowed the person he's meant to be in charge of wind up here again.

Given this dilemma, how does the procrastinator ever manage to achieve anything?
It turns out, there is one thing that scares the snot out of Instant Gratification:

Which is Panic: this is dormant most of the time, but he suddenly wakes up when a deadline comes too near or when there's a threat of public shame, a career catastrophe, or some other terrifying result.

Instant Gratification, generally unshakeable, is terrified of Panic. How else could you explain the same individual who can't seem to study for an examination from the

Shilly Shally

beginning of a semester to suddenly having the capacity to stay up all night, battling weariness, and reading

numerous pages of his textbook to complete a whole course outline? Why else would an incredibly lazy individual undertake a tough fitness regimen other than stressing out over getting less attractive?

And these are the fortunate procrastinators—some don't even react to the Panic, and in the most desperate

situations they end up fleeing, into a condition of the self-annihilating shutdown.

Quite a throng we are.

Of course, this isn't a way to live. Even for procrastinators who does manage to ultimately get things done and remain a functional member of society, something needs to change. Here are the key reasons why:

1) It's uncomfortable. Far too much of the procrastinator's valuable time is wasted toiling in the Dark Place, time

that might have been spent enjoying gratifying, well-earned relaxation if things had been done on a more reasonable timetable. And terror isn't enjoyable for anybody.

2) The procrastinator eventually sells himself short. He ends up underachieving and fails to realize his potential, which eats away at him over time and fills him with remorse and self-loathing.

3) The Have To-Dos may happen, but not the Want To-Dos. Even if the procrastinator is in a type of career where Panic is regularly present and he's able to fulfill his duties at work, the other important things in life to him—getting in shape, cooking elaborate meals, learning to play the guitar, writing a book, reading, or even making a bold career switch—never happen because Panic doesn't usually get involved with those things that seem to have no deadline. Undertakings like that broaden our experiences, make our lives richer, and provide us a lot of happiness—and for most procrastinators, they go left behind and unfulfilled.

Chapter 3

Why people Procrastinate

People frequently believe that procrastination is just a question of willpower, but truthfully, the issue is considerably more complicated.

When presented with a choice or a job to accomplish, we usually depend on our self-control to drive us in getting things done. Furthermore, our motivation, which is usually based on the hope of gaining some reward for our efforts, may help our self-control, and make it more likely that we will get things done in a timely way.

However, there are also other demotivating elements that we might face, which have an opposite impact than our motivation, meaning that they make us more prone to delay. For example, worry, fear of failure, and other negative emotions might induce us to wait needlessly, as does being assigned an unpleasant job.

Shilly Shally

Furthermore, other impeding elements interfere with our self-control and drive, in a manner that also makes us more vulnerable to procrastination. For example, tiredness, which arises as a consequence of having to work hard all day, might make it more difficult for us to exhibit self-control if it's already late at night. Similarly, a big gap between the time when we accomplish a task and the time at which we will get the reward for doing it might lead us to devalue the value of this reward, which implies that its motivating effect will be considerably decreased.

As long as our self-control and drive surpass the impacts of demotivating elements, despite the limiting variables that interfere with them, we manage to get our tasks done in a timely way. However, when all the negative influences exceed our self-control and drive, we end up procrastinating, by putting off our task either eternally, or until some future point in time when the balance flips in our favor.

Overall, we procrastinate because our self-control and drive, which could be impeded by circumstances such as weariness and incentives that are distant in the future, are

Shilly Shally

overwhelmed by demotivating ones, such as worry and fear of failure.

This causes us to fail in self-regulating our behavior, meaning that we postpone things unnecessarily, knowing fully well we should be doing them, which is why procrastination often leads to gaps between our intended actions and how we finally act in reality.

Note: there are exceptions to this, in cases where procrastination is driven by other factors, such as being rebellious or having the desire to add excitement to very boring work.

Shilly Shally

Reasons for procrastination

This section contains comprehensive lists of the specific reasons why people procrastinate, based primarily on the psychological mechanism which was outlined in the previous section.

If you're wondering why you procrastinate, check over this list, and attempt to find out which of these reasons for procrastination apply to you. Try to be thoughtful and honest with yourself as you do this because understanding the underlying causes of your procrastination is vital if you want to be able to effectively overcome it.

Note that not everything below will apply to you, so feel free to scan through the list, and read solely about factors that you believe may apply in your unique case.

Shilly Shally

Abstract aims

People are more inclined to postpone when their objectives are ambiguous or abstract, compared to when their goals are precise and well stated.

For example, objectives such as "get fit" or "start exercising" are somewhat imprecise, and are thus prone to contribute to procrastination. Conversely, goals such as "go to the gym Monday, Wednesday, and Friday directly after work, and spend at least 30 minutes on the treadmill, jogging at high speed" is tangible, and is thus far more likely to motivate you to take action.

Furthermore, consider that in addition to a lack of a clear description, other variables might make a goal seem abstract. For example, according to construal-level theory, objectives that are seen as very implausible are also perceived as somewhat abstract. This implies that if a person thinks it improbable that they would reach a given objective, this might drive them to perceive that goal as abstract, which in turn can raise the probability that they will procrastinate on it.

Shilly Shally

Outcomes that are distant in the future

People commonly procrastinate on activities that are connected with consequences (e.g., penalties or rewards) that they will only experience a while after finishing the work, as people tend to devalue the worth of results that are distant in the future. This tendency, which is predicated on the timing of results, is known as temporal discounting or delay discounting.

For example, it's simpler to minimize the worth of achieving a high score on a test when that exam is still weeks away compared to when it's just days away, which is one of the reasons why individuals wait until right before the deadline to accomplish important chores.

Accordingly, individuals frequently demonstrate a present bias when they choose to participate in activities that reward them in the short-term, at the cost of focusing on tasks that might lead to better results for them in the long run.

Note that the link between the time it takes to get a reward and the perceived value of that reward is frequently uneven, since the rate of discounting diminishes with

Shilly Shally

time. Essentially, this indicates that the further into the future a reward is, the less the increase in time counts when it comes to diminishing that prize's perceived worth.

For example, although there is a huge difference in how we value a reward that we can get now compared to a reward we can receive in a week, there is a lot smaller differences in how we value rewards we receive yearly compared to rewards we can receive in a year plus a week. Similarly, although there is a huge difference between getting a reward in a day compared to in a year, there is less of a difference between receiving a reward in a year compared to receiving it in two years.

This is called hyperbolic discounting phenomenon, and it's contrasted with exponential discounting, which is a time-consistent model of temporal discounting, where an increased delay before receiving a reward always has the same effect on its perceived value, regardless of how far in the future it is.

Shilly Shally

A detachment from our future selves

People can postpone because they regard their future self as being separated from their present self, a condition known as temporal disjunction or temporal self-discontinuity.

For example, a person might delay when it comes to eating healthy, even when their doctor told them it's important, because the harmful impact of their present diet will only start becomming a serious issue in a couple of years, which they view to be the problem of their future self.

This gap between the present and future self might drive individuals to delay in several ways. For example, it might drive people to assume that their present self shouldn't have to worry about the future because their future self will be the one who has to handle any chores that they postpone or deal with any penalties for failing to finish those activities on time. Similarly, it might lead individuals to assume that their present self shouldn't have to worry about getting things done now, since their future self would be the one who reaps the fruits of their activities.

Shilly Shally

An emphasis on future alternatives

People may resist taking action in the present because they want or hope to follow a more enticing path of action in the future. This mentality may lead to long-term procrastination, and continue even in circumstances when the individual who is delaying never ends up following through on their original strategy.

For example, a person may avoid starting to exercise on their own at home, because they plan to join a gym and start a detailed workout plan later, even though getting started now would still be beneficial and wouldn't prevent them from switching to a more serious exercise plan in the future.

Shilly Shally

Optimism or pessimism

People may delay chores because they are unduly optimistic about their capacity to fulfill such activities in the future. For example, a student could opt to postpone getting started on a project that is due a few weeks from now, since they believe that there would be lots of time to get it done later.

In many cases, this form of optimism may occur as a result of underestimating the time it will take in completing the tasks in question; this is known as the planning fallacy, and it can lead both procrastinators as well as non-procrastinators to assume that they will finish upcoming tasks earlier than they actually will.

Similarly, a person could decide, after trying to get started on a job, to postpone it until the following day, because they feel that tomorrow they will be able to force themselves to work on it, even though they have postponed the same assignment, in the same way, numerous times in the past. In many circumstances, this sort of optimism entails an overestimation of future skills, and it's crucial to note that individuals who are prone to procrastination frequently pledge to themselves that

Shilly Shally

"things will be different next time" when it comes to delaying duties.

However, pessimism may also encourage individuals to procrastinate in other situations, such as when it leads them to assume that their efforts to accomplish work are destined to fail, therefore there's no sense in beginning in the first place.

Shilly Shally

Indecisiveness

People may postpone because they are unable to make judgments in a timely way. This may be a problem in numerous ways, such as when a person can't select which course of action to participate in, or when a person has to make a precise choice before they can go on with their overall plan of action.

For example, a person can postpone beginning to diet, since they can't select which diet plan to follow. Similarly, a person can postpone getting started on their research paper, since they can't select which subject to write about.

Numerous elements typically make it more probable that someone may become trapped over-thinking the issue when attempting to make a decision, a condition which is frequently referred to as analysis paralysis or choice paralysis. The essential elements to consider, from a practical standpoint, are the following:

Shilly Shally

The more alternatives you have, the tougher it will be for you to pick. Essentially, the more alternatives you have to pick from, the tougher it will be for you to assess them and determine which one is preferred. The more similar your selections are to one another, the tougher it will be for you to pick. Essentially, the similar the available options are, and the closer they are in value, the harder it will be for you to decide which one seems better, especially in cases where no single options that is preferable to others. The more important the choice is, the more difficult it becomes to choose. in, the greater the consequences of making a particular decision, the harder it will be to finalize your decision, so you're generally likely to delay more before making major decisions than you are before making minor ones.

In addition, it's important you keep in mind that each time you have to make decisions, you end up depleting your mental resources to some extent, especially if you're prone to indecisiveness. Accordingly, the more decisions you make during a certain period, the more deplete your capacity for self-control and the more likely you're to procrastinate in making future decisions, at least until you'll have chances to refill yourself mentally.

Shilly Shally

Finally, this form of procrastination is generally referred to as decisional procrastination since it involves delays in making decisions. It's therefore contrasted with behavioral procrastination, which involves a delay in performing a task once you've decided on your preferred course of action.

Shilly Shally

Feeling overwhelmed

People may delay because they feel overwhelmed concerning the chores that they need to do. A sensation of overwhelm may develop due to a variety of factors, such as having a single duty that seems big in terms of scope or having a large number of tiny chores that build up. When this occurs, a person could just opt to ignore the duties in issue, or they might try to do them, but then wind up feeling paralyzed before those chores are accomplished.

For example, if you need to fix up your whole home, the fact that the activity would take so long and entail so many elements can lead you to feel overwhelmed, in which case you might avoid getting started on it in the first place.

Shilly Shally

Anxiety

People may procrastinate because they feel concerned about a task that they need to accomplish.

For example, someone who is concerned about checking their bills could frequently postpone doing so, even if this avoidance won't make the problem go away.

This issue can be problematic especially in cases where a person's anxiety increases resulting from their procrastination, which can lead to a feedback loop where a person feels anxious about certain task, it causes them to procrastinate instead of working on it, this makes them more anxious, and in turn causes them to procrastinate more further.

Shilly Shally

Task aversion

People sometimes postpone because they are averse to the duties that they need to do.

For example, if you need to make a critical phone call to someone you despise, you can wind yourself postponing instead of simply getting it done since you don't want to speak to them.

This arises because, in general, the more individuals find a specific work distasteful, the more likely they are to want to avoid it, and hence the more likely they are to delay.

Note that numerous variables might make a person averse to a job in a manner that leads them to procrastinate on it. For example, a person could postpone because they regard a job as annoying, laborious, uninteresting, or too hard.

Shilly Shally

Perfectionism

People may postpone due to their perfectionism. Perfectionism can lead to procrastination in several ways, such as by making someone so afraid of making a mistake that they end up not taking any action at all, or by making someone so worried about publishing something without any flaws that they end up redoing their project over and over again instead of releasing it when it was initially made.

For example, a person might delay working on their thesis, because they want every line that they write down to be perfect from the start, which causes them to not write anything at all. Similarly, someone who has finished drawing a painting might repeatedly delay sending it out for feedback, because they want to make sure that it's flawless first, so they keep going over it.

While it's reasonable and understandable to want to create and publish high-quality designs, the problem starts when perfectionists aim for unattainable flawlessness, which causes them to procrastinate by giving them seemingly valid excuses for delaying.

Shilly Shally

In that regard, perfectionism doesn't always lead to procrastination, and there are even situations where a person's perfectionism can make them less likely to procrastinate, by pushing them to do a good job and complete their tasks promptly. Also Perfectionism isn't always a negative thing, it only leads to issues when it causes people to delay unnecessarily because they're overly worried about their work not being as flawless as it should.

Shilly Shally

Fear of evaluation or negative feedback

People procrastinate sometimes because they are afraid of receiving negative feedback from others or they are afraid of being evaluated.

For example, a person might delay publicizing a project that they worked on because they're worried about what other people are going to think about it.

In many circumstances, people's anxieties in this respect are overly exaggerated or unfounded, either because the odds of obtaining unfavorable feedback are minimal, or because the implications of such feedback aren't as serious as they feel.

In addition, notice that in certain instances, it's feasible for dread of assessment or fear of bad feedback to make individuals less prone to procrastinate, by driving them to get their tasks done in a timely way. Whether the effect of this dread is beneficial or bad relies on a range of aspects, such as how nervous a person feels about the approaching review, and how confident they are in their abilities to properly manage the work at hand.

Shilly Shally

Fear of failing

People typically delay because they're terrified of failing at the things that they need to do. This fear of failure may encourage procrastination in numerous ways, such as by leading individuals to delay completing a job, or by causing them to avoid getting started on a task in the first place.

For example, someone can be so scared that their company concept will fail, that they end up continuing to work on it eternally, without ever making it accessible to the public.

How fearful someone is of failing is often connected to how essential the work in question is, such that more important activities are frequently associated with greater degrees of procrastination, in circumstances where fear of failure is the primary force behind the person's delay.

Furthermore, some personality qualities, such as poor self-esteem and low self-confidence, are related to an increased fear of failure, which makes those who have these features more inclined to delay. Moreover, fear of

Shilly Shally

failure is an especially significant problem for individuals who suffer from high levels of self-doubt, particularly among those who are prone to developing negative, illogical views about their skills.

In addition, the fear of failure doesn't always cause people to procrastinate. Rather, fear of failure encourages procrastination particularly when it diminishes people's feeling of autonomy, or when individuals feel incapable of coping with a job that they're frightened to fail at. Conversely, when individuals believe that they are well equipped to cope with a given work, fear of failure may function as a motivational force, that pushes people to avoid delaying.

Finally, perfectionism, fear of negative feedback and the fear of failure, are all related strongly to each other, but one doesn't necessitate the others, now a person might be also influenced by any combination of these factors. For instance, someone might be confident in their ability to perform a task well but still worry about receiving unjustified negative feedback from others, or they might worry about failing at something even if no one else will know about it.

Shilly Shally

Self-handicapping

People may postpone as a manner of throwing hurdles in their way so that if they fail their failings might be blamed for their procrastination rather than their talents, a practice which is referred to as self-handicapping.

For example, a student can delay instead of preparing for a test, since they prefer knowing that they failed due to their procrastination, instead of knowing that they failed because they were unable to learn the content adequately.

As a consequence of this defensive mechanism, some procrastinators spend more time postponing if they think that they are likely to fail when it comes to the work at hand, particularly if they feel that failure would reflect adversely on them.

Shilly Shally

Self-sabotage

People can delay owing to their predisposition to engage in self-defeating activities, which indicates that they intentionally strive to hinder their development.

For example, a person can postpone applying for a new job, even if they know that it represented a fantastic possibility for professional growth because they believe that they don't deserve to be in a better position in life.

There are different reasons why people participate in self-sabotage, and persons who postpone for this reason tend to also engage in other sorts of related activities, such as staying away from people who treats them well.

Shilly Shally

Low self-efficacy

Self-efficacy reflects ones belief in their ability to perform actions needed to achieve their set goals. Most times, having low self-efficacy can cause a person to procrastinate.

For example, if someone is assigned a job that they don't believe they can do, they can procrastinate getting started on it, since they feel that they would most likely fail to accomplish it anyhow.

Note that persons might have varying degrees of self-efficacy concerning different areas in their lives. For instance, a person can have high levels of academic self-efficacy, but low levels of social self-efficacy, which suggests that they believe in their skills when it comes to activities that are academic, but not when it comes to social tasks.

Furthermore, self-efficacy might relate to certain activities or talents. The most significant among them, in this context, is self-efficacy with your capacity to self-

Shilly Shally

regulate your behavior, to get yourself to finish tasks in a timely way.

This is because the notion that you would be unable to stop delaying might become a self-fulfilling prophecy, which pushes you to postpone in circumstances when you might have otherwise been able to get your job done on time.

Perceived lack of control

People may postpone because they feel powerless of managing the results of events in their lives.

For example, a person could postpone getting started on a project at work, if they fear that their employer would condemn it regardless of how much effort they put into it.

Though this apparent loss of control may play a role, in particular, in isolated circumstances, some individuals are more susceptible to perceiving a general lack of control than others. This issue is operationalized through the concept 'locus of control'. which is based on the degree to which people believe they have control over events and happenings in their life and around them. The locus of control is observed on a spectrum of externality and internality:

Individuals who are oriented
externally believe that they have a low degree of control over their life, and think that external factors, such as other people or their environment, influence them more strongly.

Shilly Shally

Individuals who are oriented internally believe that they have a high degree of control over their life.

Persons who are internally oriented tend to get started and finish things on time, whereas individuals who are externally oriented tend to procrastinate more, do worse on assignments, and suffer greater anxiety.

Shilly Shally

Attention deficit hyperactivity disorder (ADHD)

Some people procrastinate as a result of this disorder.

For example, a person might procrastinate because this disorder makes it hard for them to concentrate on a single task for long, especially once it gets boring, so they constantly jump from one task to another, without finishing any of them.

In general, research reveals that there is a considerable association between participating in ADHD-related activities and procrastinating. This is predicted, given the fact that many ADHD behaviors may lead directly to procrastination, and given that different types of procrastinatory behaviors are often seen as primary indicators of ADHD.

However, remember that not all kinds of ADHD are equally connected with procrastination, and research on the issue shows that symptoms of ADHD that have to do with inattention are more strongly associated with procrastination than symptoms that have to do with hyperactivity or impulsivity.

Shilly Shally

Depression

Some individuals procrastinate owing to underlying depression. This is because depression may lead to concerns such as exhaustion, trouble in concentration, and diminished interest in activities, which in turn can drive individuals to postpone.

For example, someone depressed might repeatedly postpone cleaning their room or going out to get groceries, because they simply don't have enough mental energy.

Shilly Shally

Lack of motivation

People typically postpone because they are not inspired enough to work on a specific assignment.

For example, a student can delay when it comes to preparing for a test on a topic that isn't related to their major since they don't care about obtaining a decent score on it.

This is typically a problem when the primary motive for doing a task is extrinsic, as in the case of someone who is forced by their parents to do well in school, rather than intrinsic, as in the instance of someone who just wants to feel that they've effectively mastered the information. Accordingly, when individuals are motivated to finish a given activity by an external source of motivation, they often demonstrate greater degrees of procrastination than when they are driven by an internal and autonomous source of motivation.

Furthermore, there are several other reasons why individuals might feel uninspired to work on a job. For example, in some circumstances, individuals feel

Shilly Shally

uninspired because they don't value the reward for executing the activity, or because they sense a gap between the task that they need to complete and the reward that is linked with it.

Finally, consider that various individuals have varying degrees of general accomplishment motivation, which indicates that some people are more driven and motivated than others to pursue their objectives in life. Accordingly, persons who have lower levels of accomplishment motivation are more inclined to delay numerous activities.

Shilly Shally

Lack of energy

People are often more inclined to delay if they suffer from low energy levels, in terms of physical or mental energy.

For example, someone who is weary after having worked hard all day could find it difficult to practice self-control when they arrive home late at night, which might lead them to procrastinate on tasks they need to take care of such as cleaning the dishes.

Shilly Shally

Laziness

Laziness represents a person's fundamental reluctance to put in the work required to attain their objectives, even when they can do so. In certain circumstances, a person's laziness might be one of the driving causes behind their procrastination.

For example, someone could delay when it comes to cleaning the dishes since they just don't feel like getting up and doing it.

However, notice that in many circumstances, individuals could believe that their procrastination is motivated by laziness, but in fact, it's happening due to some other underlying cause, such as worry or fear of failure.

In addition, observe that while laziness and lack of drive look similar, they are two independent concerns. For example, it's conceivable for someone to be very driven to pursue a given goal, but at the same time not make any progress toward it because they're reluctant to put in the required effort.

Shilly Shally

Prioritization of short-term mood

People sometimes delay because they prioritize their sentiments in the present, and do activities that will make them feel better right now, even if this comes at the price of taking action that corresponds with their long-term objectives, a phenomenon which is known as short-term mood repair.

For example, a student can procrastinate getting started on an assignment by squandering hours on hobbies like surfing social media, playing video games, and watching TV, since doing so is more enjoyable in the short term than concentrating on the subject at hand.

Essentially, this form of procrastination, is sometimes referred to as hedonistic delay, occurs when people give in to their desire for instant gratification and engage in behaviours that are satisfying in the short-term, instead of working on the tasks that will benefit them more in the long-term.

Shilly Shally

This sort of conduct corresponds to the idea of the pleasure principle, which is the inclination to seek out enjoyable activities and avoid unpleasant ones. While this propensity is normal and instinctual, it becomes a severe problem when a person is unable to control it, as it encourages them to repeatedly seek short-term happiness, at the price of long-term performance and progress.

Shilly Shally

The low ability for self-control

Self-control represents a person's capacity to self-regulate their behavior to bring oneself to follow through on their objectives, and take action that is in their best benefit, especially in the long-term. A lack of self-control makes individuals far more prone to postpone, which is not unexpected, given that self-control is vital when it comes to helping people to self-regulate their behavior.

For example, a person with poor self-control could surf social media for hours, while repeatedly telling himself that they'll get started on their job in just a few minutes, even though there is no need for them to wait.

Lack of self-control may lead individuals to delay in itself, and can also make them more inclined to postpone as a consequence of other concerns, such as work aversion or fear of failure.

Note that, in many circumstances, lacking self-control might drive individuals to participate in behaviors that are simple and accessible, even if they're not naturally

Shilly Shally

desirable, instead of focusing on things that are more intrinsically appealing, but which would need more effort. For example, a lack of self-control might cause individuals to surf the internet or social media instead of working on their favorite project, even if they don't gain much pleasure from doing so, and even though they would feel better if they were working on their preferred project.

Shilly Shally

Lack of perseverance

Perseverance is the capacity to sustain goal-driven action in the face of adversity. A lack of endurance makes individuals more prone to delay, particularly when it comes to completing projects that they've already begun working on.

For example, a lack of tenacity might force someone to quit working on their favorite side project, since they believe that they've reached a point in development that is tough and demanding.

Shilly Shally

Impulsivity

Impulsivity is the propensity to act on a whim, without planning or contemplating the implications of your actions. Impulsivity is highly related to the propensity to delay, as the choice to postpone is frequently an impulsive one, such as when individuals overlook the long-term ramifications of their actions, or when they fail to organize their work ahead of time.

For example, an impulsive person can end up procrastinating on an assignment that they're presently working on, by suddenly choosing to go out with friends, even though the project is due soon and they need to work on it now if they want to be able to turn it in on time.

Shilly Shally

Distractibility

Distractibility is the inability to concentrate your attention on one item at a time or to remain focused for a long in general. High degrees of distractibility may make a person more inclined to delay, such as when they drive individuals to frequently transfer from one center of attention to another.

For example, a person who is preparing for a test can wind up delayed because they are continuously distracted by the alerts on their phone. Similarly, someone could postpone completing numerous tasks that they began working on since they are constantly being sidetracked by ideas for intriguing new initiatives.

Shilly Shally

Sensation seeking

People may delay because they want to wait until just before the deadline to start working on things, to add pressure, difficulty, and excitement to such chores.

For example, a student could wait until the night before a class presentation is due to start working on it since they believe that doing so would make the usually monotonous job of preparing the presentation more interesting.

In certain situations, this sort of delay may lead to favorable consequences, such as when it inspires a person to work hard on a job that they would otherwise find dull. However, in most circumstances, this type of delay leads to bad effects in terms of performance. Furthermore, delaying duties, for this reason, may frequently raise the amount of stress that individuals feel, and can also impede their performance in circumstances where the delay means that they don't have enough time to cope with any unanticipated challenges that they meet in their job.

Shilly Shally

Note that some researchers refer to this procrastination that happens for this reason as arousal procrastination, in contrast with avoidant procrastination. However, this difference has been disputed, and it's not important to comprehend it from a practical standpoint, as long as you realize that this is a reason why some individuals postpone.

Shilly Shally

Rebellion

People often procrastinate as an act of rebellion, either in general or against some type of control (e.g., against an authorized person), by delaying a task that they detest being assigned.

For example, an office worker can delay an assignment that they received at work, because they despise their employer, and because they resent the fact that their supervisor sets their deadlines for them.

Similarly, individuals may delay for comparable reasons, such as retribution and anger, especially on things that they're not necessarily assigned explicitly as duties, such as going to bed.

Chapter 4

Procrastination-Action Line

You cannot depend on long-term repercussions and rewards to encourage the Present Self. Instead, you have to discover a means to transfer future incentives and penalties into the current instant. You have to make the future repercussions become current consequences.

This is precisely what occurs at the time when we finally transcend beyond procrastination and take action. For example, let's imagine you have a report to write. You've known about it for weeks and persisted to put it off day after day. You get a tiny amount of nagging discomfort and anxiety thinking about this paper you have to write, but not enough to do something about it. Suddenly, the day before the deadline, the future repercussions morph into current ones, and you compose that report hours before it is due. The agony of procrastination eventually rose and you passed the "Action Line."

Shilly Shally

There is something crucial to mention here. As soon as you pass the Action Line, the agony starts to lessen. Being in the thick of procrastinating is frequently more unpleasant than being in the middle of performing the task.

The guilt, shame, and worry that you experience when delaying are frequently greater than the effort and energy you have to put in while you're working. The trouble is not performing the job, it's beginning the task.

If we want to quit procrastinating, then we need to make it as simple as possible for the Present Self to get started and trust that inspiration and momentum will arrive once we begin. (Motivation frequently comes after the beginning, not before.)

Let's talk about how to achieve that immediately.

Shilly Shally

How to Stop Procrastinating

There are variety of strategies we can seemingly employ to stop procrastinating. Below, are outlined and explained concepts, then I'll provide you with some examples of strategy in action.

Option A: Make the Rewards of Taking Action More Immediate

If you can find a method to make the rewards of long-term decisions more immediate, then it becomes simpler to resist procrastinating. One of the finest methods to bring future benefits into the present moment is via a tactic known as temptation bundling.

Temptation bundling is a notion that developed out of behavioral economics research undertaken by Katy Milkman at The University of Pennsylvania. Simply expressed, the method advises that you combine a behavior that is healthy for you in the long run with a behavior that feels good in the short run.

Shilly Shally

The fundamental formula is: Only do [THINGS YOU LOVE] when doing [THINGS YOU ARE PROCRASTINATE ON].

Here are a few frequent instances of temptation bundling:

Only listen to audiobooks or podcasts you enjoy while exercising. Only get a pedicure while processing outstanding business emails. Only watch your favorite program while ironing or doing other home chores. Only dine at your favorite restaurant while doing your monthly meeting with a troublesome coworker.

Shilly Shally

Option B: Making the Consequences of Procrastination More Immediate

There are vast ways to force you to pay the costs of procrastination sooner than later. For instance, if you're exercising alone, skipping your workout sessions won't impact your life much at all. Your health won't deteriorate almost immediately because you've missed that one workout. The cost of procrastinating on exercising only becomes painful after days, weeks and months of being lazy towards working out. However, if committed to working out with a friend at 6 a.m. next Saturday, then the cost of skipping your workout becomes more immediate. Miss this one workout and you'll look like a total jerk.

Another common strategy is to use apps to place a bet. If you don't do what you've said you'll do, then the money goes to a charity you dislike. The objective here is to put some momentum in the game and establish new consequences that would arise if you don't conduct the behavior right now.

Shilly Shally

Option C: Designing Future Actions

One favorite tool psychologists uses to overcome procrastination is called "commitment device." Commitment devices helps you stop procrastinating by designing your future actions ahead of time.

For example, you can put a stop to your future eating habits by purchasing food in individual packages rather than in bulk sizes. You can also stop wasting time on your phone or system by deleting games or social media apps that would make you unproductive.

Similarly, you may also decrease the probability of mindless channel surfing by putting your TV in a closet and only pulling it out on major game days. You may voluntarily seek to be included in the prohibited list at casinos and online gambling sites to avoid future gambling sprees. You may develop an emergency fund by setting up an automatic transfer of monies to your savings account. These are all instances of commitment devices that can lessen the chances of procrastination.

Shilly Shally

Option D: Make the Task More Achievable

As we have previously examined, the friction that causes procrastination generally is concentrated around commencing an activity. Once you begin, it's frequently less uncomfortable to keep working. This is one solid reason to lower the size of your habits because if your habits are tiny and simple to start, then you will be less likely to delay.

One of my favorite strategies to make habits simpler is to apply The 2-Minute Rule, which says, "When you start a new habit, it should take less than two minutes to do." The aim is to make it as simple as possible to get started and then trust that momentum will drive you farther into the activity when you begin. Once you start doing something, it's easy to continue doing it. The 2–Minute Rule tackles procrastination and laziness by making it so simple to start taking action that you can't say no.

Shilly Shally

Another fantastic technique to make jobs more manageable is to divide them down. For example, take the astonishing output of the legendary writer Anthony

Trollope. He authored 47 novels, 18 pieces of non-fiction, 12 short tales, 2 plays, and a collection of essays and correspondence. How did he do it? Instead of assessing his progress based on the completion of chapters or books, Trollope monitored his progress in 15-minute increments. He established a target of 250 words every 15 minutes and he followed this routine for three hours each day. This strategy enabled him to experience emotions of pleasure and achievement every 15 minutes while continuing to concentrate on the big goal of writing a book.

Making your objectives more doable is vital for two reasons.

Small measurements of progress assist to retain momentum over the long run, which means you're more likely to accomplish major jobs. The sooner you perform a productive activity, the more rapidly your day creates an attitude of productivity and effectiveness.

I have found this second factor, the quickness with which you accomplish your first work of the day, to be of special relevance for overcoming procrastination and sustaining a highly productive output day after day.

How to Kick the Procrastination Habit
Being Consistent:

Alright, we've explored a range of ways for combating procrastination daily. Now, let's review some techniques to make productivity a long-term habit and avoid procrastination from coming back into our life.

Chapter 5

Recommended Daily Routine, for Peak Productivity

One reason it is so easy to lapse back into procrastination time after again is that we don't have a clear strategy for selecting what is essential and what we should focus on first. (This is just another example of the system frequently being more essential than the purpose.)

One of the best productivity strategies I've discovered which is also one of the most basic. It's called The 'Ivy Lee Method' comprising of six steps:

After each work day, jot down the six most critical tasks you need to achieve tomorrow. Do not write down more than six assignments. Prioritize those six things in order of their genuine relevance. When you come tomorrow, focus exclusively on the first job. Work until the first work is accomplished before moving on to the second assignment. Approach the remainder of your list in the

Shilly Shally

same method. At the end of the day, transfer any undone things to a new list of six activities for the next day. Repeat this technique every working day.

Here's what makes it so effective:

It's simple enough to work. The fundamental objection to approaches like this one is that they are too simple. They don't account for all of the complexity and subtleties of life. What happens if an emergency shows up? What about utilizing the newest technologies to our maximum advantage? In my experience, complexity is sometimes a weakness since it makes it difficult to get back on track. Yes, crises and unexpected diversions will come. Ignore them as much as you can, deal with them when you must, and go back to your priority to-do list as quickly as feasible. Use basic principles to govern complicated behavior.

It drives you to make difficult judgments. I don't think there is anything magical about Lee's number of six vital

Shilly Shally

jobs each day. It might just as well be five chores each day. However, I do believe there is something beautiful

about placing restrictions upon oneself. I think that the single greatest thing to do when you have too many ideas (or when you're overwhelmed by all you need to get done) is to prune your ideas and clip away anything that isn't required. Constraints may make you better. Lee's strategy is comparable to Warren Buffett's 25-5 Rule, which forces you to concentrate on only five vital activities and dismiss everything else. ', if you commit to nothing, you'll be distracted by everything.

It eliminates the friction of the beginning. The largest impediment to completing most projects is beginning them. (Getting off the couch might be challenging, but once you start jogging it is much simpler to accomplish your exercise.) Lee's strategy compels you to decide on your first assignment the night before you go to work. This method has proven tremendously valuable for me: as a writer, I may spend three or four hours discussing what I should write about on a given day. If I decide the night before, though, I can wake up and start writing instantly.

Shilly Shally

It's simple, yet it works. Firstly, getting started is just as crucial as succeeding.

It needs you to single-task. Modern civilization enjoys multi-tasking. The misconception about multi-tasking is that being busy is linked with being better. The precise opposite is true. Having fewer priorities leads to better work. Study world-class specialists in practically every field—athletes, artists, scientists, teachers, CEOs—and you'll notice one feature runs across all of them: attention. The rationale is straightforward. You can't be outstanding at one activity if you're always splitting your time ten different ways. 'Mastery demands attention and consistency.

Regardless matter what strategy you employ; the basic line is this: Do the most essential item first each day and allow the momentum of the first work to carry you into the next one.

Shilly Shally

Avoiding Chronic Procrastination with Visual Cues

Another strategy to resist the trap of chronic procrastination is utilizing visual signals to help activate your behaviors and asses your progress.

A visual cue is a visual reminder (anything you can see) that inspires you in taking action. And here's why they are vital for combating procrastination:

Visual signals propels you to start a habit. We frequently mislead ourselves about our capacity to remember to conduct a new behavior. ("I'm going to start eating healthier. For real this time.") A few days later, though, the drive disappears, and the hustle of life starts to take over again. Hoping you will just remember to execute a new habit is frequently a formula for failure. This is why a visual stimulus may be so beneficial. It is much simpler to continue with excellent habits when your environment correctly nudges you.

Shilly Shally

Visual signals reflect your progress on an activity. Everyone knows consistency is a key component of success, but few people truly assess how consistent they are in real life. Having a visible cue—like a calendar that monitors your progress—avoids that problem since it is a built-in measurement system. One look at your calendar then immediately you have a measure of your progress.

Visual cues may have an additive influence on motivation. As the visible proof of your success rises, it is natural to feel more driven to maintain the practice. The more visible progress you notice, the more motivated you will get to accomplish the assignment. Several popular behavioral economics studies refer to this as the Endowed Progress Effect. Seeing previous progress is a great way to trigger your next productive action.

Two of my favorite strategies that use visual cues are The Paper Clip Strategy, which helps beat procrastination day after day, and The Seinfeld Strategy, which is great for maintaining consistency over longer periods.

Shilly Shally

When it comes to anti-procrastination techniques, these are examples of relevant ones that you can use:

Prioritizing tasks based on level of importance.

Cut in bits large and overwhelming tasks into actionable pieces.

Get started on tasks by adhering to only working on them for few minutes.

Remove distractions from and around your work environment.

Identify your most and least productive times, and schedule your tasks accordingly.

Set deadlines intermediately for yourself on your route to your end objectives.

Create a daily goals and mark streak days in which you've successfully accomplished it.

Shilly Shally

Give yourself Rewards when you've successfully implemented your plan of action.

Focus on your goals instead of the tasks that you have to complete.

Visualize your future self

experiencing the outcomes of your work.

Countdown to fifteen before indulging the impulse to procrastinate.

Avoid the perfectionist mindset, therefore accept that your work will certainly not be flawless.

Believe in your ability to successfully overcome your procrastination, and that's one thing only you can do.

Conclusion

Understanding why individuals procrastinate is useful, as it may help you discover why you too procrastinate, which in turn can help you figure out how to address your procrastination issue.

Turns out there are two kinds of procrastination,

Procrastination with deadlines:
In this scenario, it turns out that when there is a deadline the consequences of procrastination are controlled because panic sets in, and results may still be attained.

The second sort of procrastination is procrastination without deadlines:
If you want to have a career, a self-starter, something entrepreneurial when there is no deadlines on those things, at first nothing is happening not until you go out and have done the hard work to get the momentum to get things going, there's also other things outside your career

Shilly Shally

that don't involve any deadline like seeing your family exercising or taking care of your health, working on your relationship or getting out of your relationship that isn't working, now if procrastinators only mechanism of doing hard things is when there is deadline and panic sets in, then that's a problem because in all of this non deadlines situations the panic doesn't show up because it has nothing to wake up for so the effects of procrastination are not contained it just extends outward forever and it's this kind of long term procrastination that is much less visible and less much talked about its usually suffered quietly and privately and it can be the source of a huge amount of long term unhappiness and regrets.

Long term procrastination would make you feel like a spectator at times in your own life, the frustration is not that you couldn't attain your ambitions but would be that you weren't even able to start pursuing them.

Shilly Shally

I don't believe non-procrastinator exists, I think all of us are procrastinators, we may not all be a mess, and some of us may have a healthy relationship with deadlines, but remember that it is sneakiest when there aren't any deadlines. we need to think about what we are procrastinating about because everyone is procrastinating on something in life, we need to stay aware of instant Gratification, that's a job for all of us, so we must start today because they aren't any more life to live than that which we already have.

Printed in Great Britain
by Amazon